MONEY AS GRAVITY

TWELVE STORIES OF MONEY, MINDSET & FINANCIAL FREEDOM

LAHSANN C. ROGERS

Money as Gravity

Twelve Stories of Money, Mindset & Financial Freedom

By Lahsann Rogers

This is a work of nonfiction. Any resemblance to actual persons, living or dead, is purely coincidental unless otherwise noted.
ISBN: 9798315918776 (PBBW)
Cover Design by: Lahsann C Rogers, Music Only Records Entertainment Company, Golden Glow Films
Interior Layout by: Lahsann C Rogers, Music Only Records Entertainment Company, Golden Glow Films
Published by Music Only Records Entertainment Company, Golden Glow Films
Printed in United States Of America
For publishing inquiries: www,joinmusiconlyrecords.com
Musiconlyrecords@gmail.com

Dedication

To **God**,
for always providing, guiding, and sustaining me—even when I couldn't see the way. Your grace is the foundation of everything I am and everything I build.

To my **son**,
you are my reason, my reflection, and my future. May this book be one of the many blueprints I leave behind to help guide your steps.

To my **mother**,
who gave every penny she could to make sure I had a chance. Your sacrifice lit the fire in me.

To my **father**,
who showed me the importance of keeping money—not just making it. Your example gave me discipline.

To my **grandmother**,
who lived far below her means, quietly liquid, always steady. You taught me that wealth isn't loud—it's wise.

To my **siblings and family**,
who have worked hard and smart, invested, failed, and invested again. You are proof that resilience builds real legacy. I've learned from your trials as much as my own, and I will continue to build forward—with love, gratitude, and purpose.

And finally To my **partner my son's mother Jillian.**

This book is for all of you..

Thank you for shaping me.

Table of Contents

Preface

This book isn't just about money.
It's about **mindset, mistakes, and movement**—the kind that shifts generations.

I didn't write this as a guru or someone who always got it right. I wrote this as someone who lived it. Someone who studied business, passed industry exams, worked on Wall Street, owned property, lost money, made it back, and still found myself wondering at times how I'd make it through the next day.

I've seen wealth built. I've seen it lost.
I've been in rooms where people made six figures a month—and I've sat at kitchen tables wondering how to make a few dollars stretch.
The difference between those two realities isn't luck—it's **knowledge, discipline, and action**.

Each chapter in this book is a story. A lesson. A blueprint.
They're not just characters—they're mirrors, composites of people I know, love, and have learned from.
Some started with less. Some made more and still ended up broke. But all of them grew once they understood one thing:

> **It's not about how much you make—it's about how much you keep, protect, and allow to grow.**

If you've ever struggled with debt, spent too much trying to look successful, avoided budgeting, feared investing, or didn't know who to ask for help—this book is for you.

And if you're already building wealth and want to go further, protect what you've built, or teach the next generation—this book is for you, too.

I wrote this so **you don't have to figure it out alone.**

So take these lessons. Highlight what hits. Pass it on when you're done. Because wealth isn't just what you hold—it's what you **leave behind**.

Let's build something worth passing down.

—

Lahsann C. Rogers

Book 1:

The Cost of Living vs. The Price of Freedom

Giorgi believed he had made it. He wore custom-tailored suits, drove a new luxury car every year, and dined at the finest restaurants without glancing at the price. His apartment sat high above Manhattan, a glass-walled penthouse that screamed status. He had the expensive watch collection, the private club memberships, and the title—corporate attorney pulling in $275,000 a year. On paper, he was a success story. But behind the lifestyle was a truth few knew: at the end of every month, Giorgi was barely breaking even.

Two weeks before, he had dined at MASA, one of New York's most exclusive Michelin-starred restaurants, where the bill for dinner alone ran nearly $2,000. But that wasn't the full picture. Valet and garage fees added another $100. His custom-tailored suit for the night cost $3,500. And his date's salon appointment—hair, makeup, and styling—came to $250. All in all, the night cost him $5,850. It was just one night, but it wasn't the first—and it wouldn't be the last. The deeper problem wasn't the price of dinner—it was the price of trying to look like he had everything under control.

Giorgi had convinced himself that his lifestyle was justified by his income. But in truth, he was spending faster than he was saving. Chasing image, not impact. Status, not freedom. His credit card debt had ballooned to $75,000 across multiple accounts, each carrying punishing interest rates. He leased luxury cars that drained his account monthly. His rent alone was $7,500, and yet he had little to nothing invested or saved. Despite earning more than many households combined, Giorgi was living paycheck to paycheck—just at a more glamorous level.

Things came to a head when his firm announced a freeze on raises and bonuses. It wasn't a layoff, but it was a reality check. For the first time, Giorgi looked at the numbers with sober eyes. He had no emergency fund. His 401(k) was barely touched. His net worth? Negative. One job loss could

mean complete collapse. He realized that he was one financial shock away from losing it all.

As Dave Ramsey once said, "Too many people buy things they don't need with money they don't have to impress people who don't care." Giorgi was finally ready to stop performing wealth and start building it. He downsized his apartment, saving thousands every month. He returned his leased car and bought a reliable used vehicle outright. He created a strict budget and stuck to it, tracking every dollar. He tackled his debt aggressively using the snowball method and balance transfers. He began investing consistently and finally maxed out his 401(k). Most importantly, he studied how to build streams of passive income—dividend-paying stocks, index funds, and cash-flowing assets that could help him earn money in his sleep.

Giorgi no longer worked just to maintain a lifestyle. He worked to build something real. As Warren Buffett famously said, "If you don't find a way to make money while you sleep, you will work until you die." Giorgi stopped chasing approval and started chasing freedom.

He had to admit—he never used to think about the numbers clearly. Everything felt affordable in the moment. But the math told the truth. Giorgi's annual income was $275,000. That broke down to about $22,916.67 per month, $5,288.46 per week, and just $753.42 per day. On the night he dined at MASA, Giorgi had spent $5,850. That was more than an entire week of income. It was nearly eight times more than what he earned in a single day. And if that kind of spending became even remotely regular, the numbers got worse.

Spending $5,850 weekly would add up to $304,200 per year—already more than his entire salary. Monthly, it would total $23,400. And if he somehow spent like that every day? That would be $2,135,250 per year. Giorgi would need eight times his current income just to keep up—and that's before taxes, rent, debt payments, or basic living costs. It was a game he couldn't win. Not without changing the rules.

The hard truth? Even a six-figure salary can't outpace reckless spending. Giorgi wasn't rich—he was overextended. He wasn't building wealth—he

was burning through his future. A big income means nothing if you're broke.

Real wealth isn't loud—it's quiet, intentional, and growing slowly in the background. Giorgi finally understood that making money was only step one. The real game was how much he kept, invested, and allowed to multiply over time. If your spending exceeds your earning, no salary will ever be enough. His story is proof that real financial power comes not from the paycheck, but from what you do with it.

Moral of the Story:
A high income means nothing if your lifestyle swallows it whole. Giorgi learned that true wealth isn't measured by what you wear, drive, or post—but by what you *keep*, *invest*, and *let grow quietly behind the scenes*. Financial freedom doesn't come from spending more. It comes from spending *less than you earn* and putting the difference to work.

Because at the end of the day, overspending is a choice—so is wealth.

Real-World Instructional: You Can't Spend More Than You Make (No Matter the Take)

Giorgi's Just-for-Show Broke Math

Let's break it down in plain, common-sense terms:

If you make $275,000 a year and spend like you make $2 million, guess what?

You're not rich. You're just in debt… with a better wardrobe.

Giorgi's mistake is one too many people make: confusing income with wealth and luxury with leverage.

It doesn't matter if you're pulling six figures or six hundred—if your outflow is greater than your inflow, you're headed for a financial faceplant.

Imagine this:

- **You make $5,000 a month.**
- **Your rent is $2,500.**
- **Your car note is $800.**
- **Your designer sneaker addiction costs you $600/month.**
- **You eat out five nights a week like Yelp is paying you.**
- **You "treat yourself" like it's your full-time job.**

Now your checking account has the audacity to hit you with that "*Insufficient Funds*" alert… and you're mad at the bank like it's their fault.

Newsflash: The math is mathing. And the math don't lie.

Just because you *can* swipe it, doesn't mean you *should*.

Real wealth isn't about how much you make—it's about how much you keep, invest, and multiply. You can't out-earn bad habits, and you definitely can't flex your way into freedom.

So if you're wondering why you're always broke at the end of the month even with a solid paycheck, the answer might not be "more money"—it might be more sense.

Remember: You can't spend more than you make… no matter the take.

Book 2:

Money Isn't Everything—The Way We Use It Is

In a quiet suburb just outside Atlanta, three college friends—**Sophia**, **Tanya**, and **Joyner**—sat on the steps of Sophia's first apartment the summer after graduation, each with a drink in hand and ambition in their eyes.

"We're going to invest," Tanya said, confidently. "No excuses. Let's see who ends up with the biggest bag."

They laughed, but they meant it. They all chose the same portfolio—a mix of strong, blue-chip, dividend-paying stocks. What differed wasn't *what* they bought, but *how* they bought it.

Tanya was the strategist. She believed in precision. "Timing is everything," she'd say. "Why buy high when you can buy low?" She only invested when markets dipped. If things were flat or rising, she held her cash, waiting for the perfect drop. Sometimes those dips never came, and her money sat untouched.

Joyner was the hype man. When the markets were booming, he was all in. He got excited when headlines buzzed and stocks hit new highs. "Let's ride the wave!" he'd text them. But as soon as things got shaky, he panicked and pulled out. He hated risk, and more than once, he sold at a loss just to feel safe.

Sophia, though, played the long game. She set up automatic transfers of $500 each month into her portfolio, no matter what the market was doing. She reinvested every dividend, never paused or skipped a contribution, even when the news was filled with fear. "Just like I pay my rent and bills," she told them, "I pay my future self."

They joked with her sometimes, called her "The Tortoise." But she didn't mind. She wasn't chasing highs—she was building slow, steady wealth.

Twenty years passed.

Now in their 40s, the trio met for brunch in midtown. Sophia picked a sunny spot near the window, Tanya slid in with fresh designer, and Joyner strolled in late with a wide grin.

"So," Tanya said, sipping her coffee. "We gonna talk numbers?"

"Let's do it," Sophia said, pulling out her phone.

Tanya was first. "I put in about $120,000 over the years," she said. "Portfolio's sitting at... around $480K. Not bad. Could've done better if I didn't wait so long between buys."

Joyner looked sheepish. "Same $120,000 for me... but I only got about $325K." He shook his head. "I was scared to buy when things were low. I guess I was too reactive."

Sophia smiled, opened her app, and turned the screen toward them.

$790,000.

Tanya leaned in. Joyner's jaw dropped.

"Eighteen thousand a year in dividends alone," Sophia added casually.

"How?" Joyner asked. "Same portfolio. Same time frame."

"It's not magic," she said. "It's just consistency and compound interest."

Tanya leaned back and nodded. "Damn."

Sophia laughed, then quoted Einstein, like she'd memorized it just for this moment.
"Compound interest is the eighth wonder of the world. He who understands it, earns it… he who doesn't, pays it."

They paused. For once, even Joyner was quiet.

Here's what Sophia had done, broken down simply: She invested $500 a month, every month, for 20 years. Her total contributions were $120,000. With an average annual return of 10%—which is what the S&P 500 has historically returned with dividends reinvested—her portfolio grew to over $790,000. While Tanya waited for dips and Joyner chased spikes, Sophia just kept buying. During market crashes, she bought more shares. During rallies, those shares grew in value. Her dividends reinvested themselves. Her portfolio didn't just grow—it **compounded**.

Over time, her discipline turned into freedom. While the guys were trying to outsmart the market, Sophia simply let time and consistency do the work.

Tanya leaned in and clinked her glass to Sophia's. "Alright, Tortoise," she said. "You won."

"No," Sophia said with a smirk, "I just stayed in the race."

Moral of the Story: Consistency wins. Tanya timed. Joyner chased. But Sophia trusted the power of compounding interest over time. By putting her money to work and letting **compound interest grow-it-quietly behind the scenes**, she didn't just invest in stocks—she invested in **freedom**. **It's not about how much you make—it's about how you use it, how consistently you invest it, and how patiently you let it grow.**

Real-World Instructional: Don't Wait—Automate & Compound Your Way to Wealth

Sophia's No-Drama, Grown-Folks Investing Game

**Let's be real. Most people treat investing like dating:
They're in when it's exciting, out when it gets tough, and ghost the whole thing the moment it gets boring.**

But Sophia? Sophia's the friend who shows up early, brings snacks, and minds her business while her money minds its growth.

Here's what Sophia did, and what most people *don't* do:

- **She invested $500 a month, like clockwork.**
- **Rain or shine, market crash or boom, recession or rally—she invested.**
- **She reinvested her dividends, didn't try to time the market, and never flinched when the headlines got spicy.**

Meanwhile:

- **Tanya was checking stock charts like they were horoscope readings, only investing when the "stars aligned."**
- **Joyner chased the hype and dipped when things got scary, like a financial horror movie with popcorn.**

And Sophia? She just let compound interest do its quiet little magic trick.

Let's run her real numbers:

- **$500/month = $6,000/year**
- **Over 20 years = $120,000 total invested**
- **With an average 10% return (S&P 500 style) and dividends reinvested?**
- **She ended up with around $790,000**
- **And $18,000/year in passive income—aka money that pays her to breathe.**

No lottery. No risky bets. No meme stocks. Just grown-up habits and consistency.

> **"You can't time the market, but you can spend time *in* the market. That's where the money lives."**

Moral of the math?
If you're waiting for the *perfect* time to start investing, you're already late.

If you're only investing when things feel good, you're gonna miss the growth.

And if you're relying on vibes instead of strategy, your portfolio might end up with the same fate as Joyner's: nervous and underfunded.

Be like Sophia. Stay consistent. Automate it. Reinvest it. Then chill.
Let time + dividends + common sense = wealth.

Book 3:

The Language of Money

Giorgi sat across from his two senior partners, a glass wall behind them casting sunlight over a polished mahogany conference table. After a decade of dedication, late nights, and seven-figure deals closed, he was finally being offered what most associates only dreamed of—**partnership**.

"You've earned this," said Brandon, the founding partner. "But as you know, there's a buy-in. It's not just a title, Giorgi. It's a seat at the table."

"$350,000," added Joanne, the managing partner. "We'll structure it, but you'd need to come up with at least half up front. We want you in—just be sure this is the path you want."

Giorgi didn't respond right away. The title sounded good. It always had. **Partner.** But something inside him stirred. It wasn't hesitation—it was evolution. He'd spent years climbing this ladder, but lately, he'd started wondering if he was even on the right one.

That night, he didn't celebrate. Instead, he met up with a local entrepreneur he'd represented in a past merger—a sharp, fast-talking man named Malik who ran multiple businesses and looked ten years younger than he was.

"I've been where you are," Malik said over their whiskey-free cocktails. "Big title, fancy office, great paycheck. But I wasn't free. I was making money, yeah—but I wasn't **moving money.** Money was working me. Not the other way around."

Giorgi leaned in. "So how'd you flip it?"

"By learning the **language of money**," Malik replied. "See, most people learn how to work. A few learn how to do business. But the wealthy? They speak money fluently. They use debt as a tool. They structure corporations, not just careers. They let taxes work in their favor. They don't just *earn*—they *build*."

That conversation lingered in Giorgi's mind for weeks.

He made an appointment with a business banker. Together, they crunched numbers, weighed risks, and explored what it would take for Giorgi to start his own law firm.

"You've got excellent credit," the banker told him. "Based on your financials and industry profile, we could approve up to $500,000 in working capital. Possibly more with collateral."

Giorgi blinked. "You'd really lend me that much?"

"You're not just a borrower," the banker said. "You're an asset."

Giorgi had never heard himself described that way. But it clicked.

He then met with an older CPA who'd run a private legal consultancy for decades. The man pulled out a napkin and drew three circles: **LLC, S-Corp, and Trust**.

"You set this up right," the CPA said, "and you'll save tens of thousands in taxes every year. Not to mention what you can write off. Your car. Your office. Some of your meals. You're building equity now, not just income."

That night, Giorgi didn't sleep. He paced. He journaled. He ran numbers. He stared at his reflection in the mirror and whispered, **"Am I building someone else's empire—or am I ready to build my own?"**

Within three months, he respectfully declined the partnership offer and launched his own boutique law firm. Small office. Two staff members. One assistant. One rented suite. It wasn't glamorous at first—but it was his.

The first year was lean, but strategic. He worked twice as hard, but this time, every client, every invoice, every hour... it all fed *his* system. He applied what he'd learned: kept his overhead low, tracked his business expenses, invested his retained earnings into dividend stocks and a SEP-IRA, and started thinking like a producer—not a professional.

By year three, Giorgi's firm was pulling in more than he had ever earned at the old firm—and with less stress. He had the flexibility to choose his cases, pick his clients, and build a culture of integrity. He wasn't just practicing law anymore—he was practicing **ownership**.

The numbers told the story best.

At his old firm:
$275,000/year salary, taxed heavily, with little equity.

At his new firm:
$600,000/year in revenue, structured through an S-Corp, paying himself a salary of $120,000 and taking the rest in distributions, which were taxed at a lower rate.
He wrote off business travel, home office upgrades, client meals, continuing education, and even a portion of his car payments.
He reinvested profits, bought into a commercial property for office space, and later began mentoring other young attorneys looking to go solo.

He wasn't just **earning** anymore—he was **building**. The language of money no longer intimidated him. He spoke it fluently.

As he once heard someone say:

> "Money: a tool used for trade, survival, and investment. It holds no power until you control how it moves."

And he now knew:
Business is the structure.
Work is the value.
A career is a path.
But **ownership**—ownership is power.

Most people spend their lives working for money. Giorgi had finally learned how to **make money work for him**.

Moral of the Story:
Giorgi had the title, the salary, and the respect—but not the freedom. When he stopped working *in* the system and started building his own, he discovered the

true power of money: **ownership**. The wealthy don't just earn more—they structure better, invest smarter, and understand how to make every dollar speak.

He didn't just change his career—he changed the conversation.

The real flex isn't partnership. It's control and tax breaks.

Real-World Instructional: Starting Your Own Business, Offering a Service & Taking Control

So you're thinking of doing your own thing? Good. Let's talk sense.

Starting your own business isn't about being a boss for Social Media—it's about taking control of your **income**, your **time**, and your **taxes**.

Let's start with this simple truth:
If you have a **skill, talent, or service** people need—you already have a business. You just haven't packaged it yet.

Giorgi was a lawyer. His product was his expertise. But this applies whether you're a barber, accountant, coach, editor, designer, therapist, or anyone offering value.

Here's how to get started without the fluff:

✅ Step 1: Register Your Business

Start an **LLC** or **S-Corp** in your state. This gives you legal structure and opens the door to tax benefits, business credit, and legitimacy.

- Need help? Use services like LegalZoom or your state's business portal.
- Bonus: Your business name is now official. Let that sink in.

✅ Step 2: Separate Your Money

Open a **business checking account** and never mix it with your personal funds. Track everything: income, expenses, invoices. This isn't just good practice—it's your foundation for real control.

✅ Step 3: Offer Your Service & Solve a Problem

Your business only needs one thing to start: a customer with a problem.

- Giorgi didn't wait to build a skyscraper. He rented a small office, hired two people, and offered the exact same services he'd been doing at the big firm—just under his own name.
- You don't need 1,000 clients. You need 5 loyal ones to start.

✅ Step 4: Use the Tax Code Like the Wealthy Do

Business owners write off what employees can't.

- Office rent? Write-off.
- Business meals? Partially deductible.
- Marketing, subscriptions, software, even your **phone bill**—potentially deductible.
- That trip to meet a client? Business mileage.

As an employee, your taxes come out first.
As a business owner, your expenses come out first—**then** you pay taxes on what's left.
That's not a loophole. That's structure.

✅ Step 5: Pay Yourself Like a Pro

If you're set up as an S-Corp, pay yourself a **reasonable salary**, then take the rest in **distributions**, which are often taxed at a lower rate.
Set up retirement accounts like a **SEP IRA** or **Solo 401(k)**—you'll save for the future and lower your tax bill now.

Common Mistakes to Avoid

- **Waiting until everything's "perfect."** Just start. You'll learn more in motion than in theory.

- **Spending too much up front.** Start lean. Focus on service and systems—not flash.
- **Not knowing your numbers.** A budget and a basic profit/loss spreadsheet go a long way.
- **Being afraid to charge.** You're not just charging for time. You're charging for skill, value, and transformation. Own it.

Final Word

You don't need a million-dollar idea.
You need a **service that solves a problem**, the courage to start small, and the wisdom to stay consistent.

Whether you're launching a firm like Giorgi or freelancing on weekends, the goal is the same:
Build something that works for you.

Because when you run the business—**you stop working for the check and start controlling the checkbook.**

Sidebar: Giorgi's Power Moves vs. The Desk Job Trap™

The Old Giorgi	The New Giorgi
Wore $3,500 suits to beg for bonuses	Wears polos and *cuts himself the check*
Waited on HR to "circle back"	Files his own paperwork and hires HR
Couldn't deduct his lunch	Deducts lunch *and* writes off the gas to get there
Asked for time off	*Gives* himself Fridays off (unless court's calling)

Made rich people richer	Became one of the rich people
Talked about "one day"	Signed a lease and made it **Day One**

What did we learn here?
You can stay at the table someone else built,
or you can build your own table...
and write it off on your taxes.

Book 4:

Why Saving & Investing Matter More Than Spending

In a quiet neighborhood on the edge of a small Midwestern town lived **Mr. Leon Wills**—the local school janitor. He swept halls, mopped gym floors, and polished trophy cases with the kind of pride usually reserved for CEOs and architects. He wore the same navy work jacket every day, drove a modest but clean sedan, and lived in a one-story brick home with green shutters, which he'd bought in cash decades ago.

To most people, Leon was simply "Mr. Wills"—kind, quiet, and dependable. He brought donuts to the front office once a month, waved to kids every morning, and could fix a broken faucet faster than the maintenance request could be filled out. He didn't say much, but when he did, it was always short, humble, and filled with a smile.

What no one knew—**not the principal, not the neighbors, not even his barber of 35 years**—was that Mr. Wills had quietly become a **multi-millionaire**.

His secret? He never lived above his means, and he never let money make decisions for him. He made **small, smart choices** every day—and he made them **over time**.

Leon didn't spend much. He bought what he needed, took care of it, and let it last. His house was small but well-kept. His car was reliable and paid off. His clothes were simple. His meals were home-cooked. And every paycheck, **he saved—then invested.**

He put money into **EE savings bonds and I Bonds**—low-risk, government-backed investments that slowly grew over time, compounding steadily, quietly. He invested in **dividend-paying insurance and utility stocks**, the kind that didn't make headlines but **paid out checks every quarter**. Over time, he bought **small residential properties** in the neighborhood—an extra house here, a duplex there—then placed them into a **trust**, ensuring they would be cared for long after he was gone.

He kept **no credit card debt**, avoided flashy purchases, and built up a **high-yield savings account** that reached **over $1 million** before he turned 65. He reinvested earnings, managed his expenses, and read library books on money instead of trying to impress people with it.

When Mr. Wills passed at age 92, the town gathered at his memorial with stories of kindness, cookies delivered to classrooms, lightbulbs changed for elderly neighbors, and how he never forgot a birthday. They expected a few hundred dollars to be left behind—maybe enough for flowers.

But Leon's attorney revealed the truth.

He left behind $10 million.

- **$1 million in cash**
- **$5 million in liquid investment accounts**
- **The rest in real estate—income-generating properties managed through a trust**
- All of it legally structured, **tax-efficient**, and **ready to pass on to future generations**

The beneficiaries? A mix of **family, former students, local charities, and scholarship funds for trade school students**. His wealth wasn't just money—it was a message. A legacy. A quiet reminder that **you don't have to look rich to build something priceless.**

Leon never made six figures. He just understood what most people miss: **you don't need more income—you need more discipline**.

> "The goal is not just to make money, but to ensure it stays and grows while you sleep."

He let his money rest while he worked. And eventually, his money did the working for him.

He didn't chase image. He built assets. He didn't flash cash. He built value. And when it was all said and done, Mr. Wills—the janitor with the mop and the quiet smile—taught an entire town the true definition of wealth.

Moral of the Story:
Frugality is not about being cheap—it's about being intentional. Mr. Wills didn't need to be flashy to be wealthy. By saving consistently, investing smartly, avoiding debt, and planning ahead, he built a fortune while living simply. **Wealth isn't loud—it's built in silence, protected by discipline, and revealed through legacy.**

Real-World Instructional: Building Quiet Wealth Like Mr. Wills

You don't need a corner office, flashy title, or viral business idea to build wealth.
You need **discipline, time, and intention.** Mr. Wills didn't make millions overnight—he made **smart decisions repeatedly**, over decades. You can do the same. Here's how:

---

1. Live Below Your Means

- Buy the house you *need*, not the one your ego wants.
- Drive a reliable car, not one that needs a name tag at valet.
- Avoid lifestyle purchases—when your income goes up, your spending doesn't have to follow.

---

2. Save First, Spend What's Left

- Use **automatic transfers** to move money into savings/investments before you even touch it.
- Build a 6-month **emergency fund** in a high-yield savings account.
- Pretend raises never happened—stash the difference.

---

3. Invest Like a Grown-Up

- Start with **low-risk, long-term investments**:
  - **EE Bonds, I Bonds** – great for long-term security
  - **Dividend stocks & index funds** – consistent cash flow and growth
  - **Real estate** – appreciate in value and generate rent
- Reinvest dividends and earnings like it's second nature.

📜 4. Protect What You Build

- Use **trusts** to avoid probate, reduce taxes, and control how wealth is passed on.
- Have **life insurance** to protect loved ones and create wealth beyond the grave.
- Keep your will, financial documents, and beneficiary designations up to date.

🧠 5. Remember: You Don't Have to Look Rich to *Be* Rich

- Mr. Wills had millions. People thought he had pennies.
- He wasn't trying to impress—he was trying to *impact.*
- When you live for purpose, the profits follow.

Quiet money makes loud moves... eventually.

😂 Sidebar: How to Ball Quietly Like Mr. Wills™

Things Mr. Wills Did	What People Thought	Reality
Lived in a modest one-story home	"Aww, he's just getting by."	House was paid off since 1987.
Drove a 15-year-old sedan	"That man needs a new ride."	Had six figures earning interest.
Wore the same work jacket every day	"He's humble."	He owned stock in the company that made it.
Brought donuts to the office monthly	"Such a sweet old man!"	Wrote it off as a goodwill expense.

Never talked about money	"Probably doesn't have much."	Had a trust fund and real estate empire.
Left behind $10M	"Wait… what?!"	Yep. You missed the blueprint.

Lesson?
You can flex with followers… or you can finesse with freedom.
Mr. Wills chose freedom for himself and those to come after him.

Book 5:

The Power of Budgeting & Avoiding Debt

Every dollar she earned had a job. And **Tasha** made sure it showed up to work.

She was a single mother of three, living in a cramped apartment on the south side of town. Her days started before sunrise and ended well past midnight. Her first job as a school cafeteria cook paid just enough to cover rent, lights, and a modest meal on the table. Her second job as a weekend cleaning lady kept the fridge from going empty. But it was her **side hustle**—buying and selling hair extensions online and through word of mouth—that kept her dream alive.

Tasha wasn't just working to survive. She was **grinding to escape.**

She'd been buried in student loan debt for years—loans she took to earn a degree she never got to finish. A broken engagement and two kids under five at the time forced her to put school on pause… and never look back. The interest piled on like wet laundry she never had time to fold.

But Tasha knew one thing: if she couldn't make more money, she had to **control the money she had.** Budgeting wasn't optional—it was the only way to breathe.

With a yellow notepad, a calculator from the dollar store, and a highlighter that barely worked, she created a simple but effective system:

- **Rent first. Lights second. Food third.**
- Every leftover dollar had a name: savings jar, hair inventory, debt snowball.
- She used her second job to chip away at her student loans one payment at a time.

- Her side hustle money? That was **the dream fund**—used to build inventory, fill orders, and one day… become full-time.

She never bought what she didn't need. She never used credit unless it was an emergency. Her fridge had coupons taped to the side. Her "vacations" were walks with the kids to the park. And still—**they never went without.**

Years passed. Her kids grew. So did her discipline. The hair business expanded. She got a used van to do local deliveries. She learned digital marketing on her lunch breaks. And then—one of her sons, **Jayden**, scored a full ride to college to play football.

He never forgot watching his mother hustle. He remembered her staying up braiding wigs for cash. He remembered not always having new shoes, but always having clean ones. And when he made it to the **NFL**, the first thing Jayden did—**was invest in her business.**

"Mom," he said. "You built something out of nothing. You taught me more than football ever did."

With his backing and her strategy, Tasha turned her hustle into a brand. She opened her first storefront, then her second. But the heart of the success wasn't the money—it was the method.

She still budgeted. Still tracked expenses. Still reinvested. She paid off the remainder of her debt, hired help, and built a cushion that gave her something she never had before: **peace of mind**.

And Jayden? He saw what budgeting looked like in real time. Instead of blowing his NFL checks on chains and fast cars, he lived well below his means. He invested in index funds, saved, and even opened a training facility in his hometown for young athletes—with his mother helping him manage the books.

> "Avoiding high-interest debt and sticking to a budget aren't restrictions—they are financial freedom tools."

Tasha proved that budgeting doesn't mean you're broke. It means you're **focused**.

She turned survival into structure. Hustling into strategy.
And struggle… into stability.

Moral of the Story:
Budgeting isn't about limits—it's about **liberation**. Tasha didn't have much, but she made every dollar count. By staying disciplined, managing debt, and refusing to spend more than she earned, she built not only a business—but a blueprint. She didn't just teach her son how to manage money—she showed him how to **respect it**.

Real-World Instructional: Budgeting Your Way Out of the Struggle

Budgeting isn't about being broke.
It's about telling your money where to go **before it gets lost** in nonsense.

Tasha didn't have a fancy finance degree or an app that rounded up her purchases and turned them into stock portfolios.
What she had was **discipline**, a notebook, and the **courage to live within her means** when everything around her screamed otherwise.

Here's how to build a budget when you're stretched thin and still trying to win:

💡 1. Separate Needs from Wants (For Real)

- **Need** = Rent, food, utilities, transportation, childcare
- **Want** = $12 smoothies, last-minute online sales, and "because I work hard" splurges
  If it doesn't keep the lights on or get you closer to your goals, it can wait.

📓 2. Use a Simple System You'll Actually Stick To

- The **50/30/20 Rule**:
  - 50% Needs
  - 30% Wants
  - 20% Savings or Debt
- Or go old school like Tasha:
  - A notebook
  - Envelopes or jars for cash categories
  - Or a spreadsheet that makes you feel like a boss

💳 3. Attack Debt Strategically

- Use the **snowball method**:
  - Pay off the smallest balance first for quick wins
  - Then roll those payments into the next biggest one
- Or the **avalanche method**:
  - Start with the highest interest debt
  - Save more in the long run

Either way: **pay something. Every month. On time.**

💼 4. Treat Your Side Hustle Like a Business

- Track inventory and costs
- Separate business and personal money
- Reinvest instead of spending your first big sale
- Save for slow months—it's not always booming

🧠 5. Teach What You Practice

Tasha didn't just budget—she **modeled it**.
Her kids learned through **watching her grind with grace**.
The result? A son who made millions and *still budgets like he's got a light bill due.*

📉 Sidebar: Tasha's Real-Life Budget Hacks™

"Broke" Thinking	Tasha's Budget Boss Moves
"I deserve to treat myself!"	Treated herself to *not overdrafting this week*
"Credit card now, worry later."	Budgeted now, slept later *without stress*
"If I ignore the bills, maybe they'll forget."	Put 'em on autopay and faced 'em like a champ
"I'll use my tax return to fix it."	Used her tax return to *build it*
"Budgeting is boring."	So is being broke with no backup plan. 💁🏽‍♀️

Lesson?
You don't have to make six figures to act like you've got sense.
Budget like your future depends on it—because it does.

Book 6:

Entrepreneurship, Partnerships & Passive Income

Wolf had the idea.

It came to him one night while fixing a friend's laptop on his living room floor. He'd been repairing electronics for years—phones, tablets, even gaming consoles—and doing it faster and better than the overpriced tech stores. He had no fancy certifications, but his work? Solid. Reliable. Repeat customers. And word of mouth was growing louder.

He looked across the room at his younger brother, **Zeke**, who was scrolling on his phone, still in his security guard uniform from his second job.

"Man, we could really do something with this," Wolf said.

"With what?" Zeke didn't look up.

"This. The repairs. A shop. Maybe a mobile service. People already calling me every day."

Zeke shrugged. "Yeah, but who's got startup money like that? Plus, that's risky. You know Mom would say keep the job with benefits."

"I'm not trying to work overnight shifts forever, bro. I'm talking ownership."

Zeke didn't argue. He just looked back at his phone. The conversation ended there.

A week later, Wolf ran into **Tami**, an old friend from high school. She was running a small social media marketing business and had recently launched a newsletter about local small businesses.

"You still doing tech repairs?" she asked over lunch.

"Yeah. Thinking about making it a full business," Wolf said. "Just not sure where to start."

Tami leaned forward. "You've got the hands and the skill. I've got the network. You set up the systems, I'll get the word out."

And just like that, a partnership was born.

They started small: a basic website, an Social Media page, and a $900 loan from Wolf's tax refund. Tami did the branding, marketing, and outreach. Wolf handled every repair with care and speed. Within six months, they had a mobile repair van, contracts with local schools and small businesses, and a waitlist.

They called it **FixRight Mobile Tech**.

Zeke watched it grow from the sidelines. He'd never thrown shade. But he hadn't believed in it either. Until now.

One Saturday morning, Wolf got a text:
Zeke: "You hiring?"
Wolf: "Always. Come thru Monday."

There was no "I told you so." Just a handshake, a job title, and a new business card that read: **Field Technician, FixRight Mobile Tech.**

Zeke now handled logistics and scheduling. He ended up building a client tracking system that saved them hours of admin work every week. He even helped open their second mobile unit.

> "True wealth isn't built through a salary alone. Ownership creates wealth—jobs create salaries."

What started as a disagreement became alignment.
What could've been resentment became respect.

Wolf still owned the business, and Tami remained a vital partner, receiving her share of the profits. They later brought in more help, trained new techs, and created online repair tutorials that brought in **passive income** every month from ads and subscribers. Eventually, they launched an eBook and short course for beginners looking to start mobile repair hustles in their own cities.

Zeke's contribution? A budget system and app recommendation that helped those same beginners **track profit and growth from day one**.

No drama. No family tension. Just **different paths that led back to each other**.

Moral of the Story:
Entrepreneurship isn't just about ideas—it's about execution and alignment. Wolf didn't wait for everyone to agree—he partnered with someone who believed in the vision. Later, the same brother who didn't see the dream helped scale it. **Ownership builds wealth, partnerships multiply it, and when the vision is solid, even doubters can become builders.**

Real-World Instructional: Starting Small, Partnering Smart, and Earning While You Sleep

You don’t need a million-dollar loan to start a business.
You don’t need to go viral.
You just need to start where you are—with what you have—and build up from there.
Just like Wolf.

Here’s how to get started (for real):

🛠 1. Start With a Service, Not a Storefront

- What can you do well *right now* that solves a problem?
    - Tech repair, cleaning, cooking, tutoring, photography, fitness coaching, hair styling—you name it.
- Don’t overthink it. If people are already asking you for help, you’ve got a market.

🤝 2. Find a Partnership That Adds, Not Drains

- A good partner brings what you *don’t*: marketing, systems, organization, or sales.
- Communicate upfront. What are the goals? Who owns what? How is income split?
- Pro Tip: **Write it down.** Even if you're friends. Especially if you're family.

📊 3. Track the Money Early

- Keep personal and business finances separate. Open a free business checking account.
- Track sales, expenses, and profit weekly. Use tools like Wave, QuickBooks, or even Google Sheets.
- Know how much you're making—and how much you're spending—to avoid guessing.

💡 4. Scale With Purpose

- Don't hire just because you're tired. Hire when you have systems.
- Automate repeat tasks. Save your energy for growth.
- Reinvest profits into the business, not into flexing.

💤 5. Build Passive Income Streams

Once your service is running smooth, think:

- Digital products (tutorials, templates, eBooks)
- Affiliate links for tools you use
- YouTube or TikTok tutorials with monetized content
- Subscription plans or membership models

You're not just trading time anymore—you're creating streams of income that flow **while you sleep**.

😎 Sidebar: How to Tell If You're an Owner or Just Hustling in Circles™

If You're Still...	But an Owner Would...

Fixing phones for friends "just to help out"	Set prices, invoice properly, and get paid on time 💼
Doing everything yourself with zero systems	Delegate, automate, and protect their peace 😌
Waiting for everyone to "believe in you"	Work with people who believe in your **work** 🛠
Treating your business like a hobby	Getting that LLC, EIN, and separate bank account 💳
Asking “Can I afford this?” after every sale	Checking the profit margin spreadsheet like a CEO 🧾
Blowing your first big payday on stuff you can’t write off	Reinvesting and building passive income 💰

Lesson?
Don’t wait for everyone to “get it.” Build it, brand it, and believe in it first.
Even if your own brother needs a minute—**they’ll come around when the vision is real.**

Book 7:

Your Reputation Is a Financial Asset

> "It takes 20 years to build a reputation and five minutes to ruin it. If you think about that, you'll do things differently."
> — Warren Buffett

Keisha didn't have a fancy storefront. No neon signs, no viral reels, no flashy branding kits.

But everyone in her city knew her name—and more importantly, **they trusted it**.

She was a custom event planner. Weddings, milestone birthdays, grand openings, baby showers—you name it, she made it unforgettable. Her style wasn't just creative—it was precise. She remembered allergies, respected budgets, and never promised more than she could deliver.

More than once, she turned down work that didn't align with her values.

"You could've made bank off that bachelor party," her cousin once told her.

"Yeah," Keisha replied. "And lost a client who books me for corporate galas twice a year."

She got it. **Branding wasn't just about logos and colors. It was about character.** Her clients weren't just buying decorations and planning—they were buying her **reputation**. Her name carried weight in boardrooms, bridal parties, and neighborhood Facebook groups.

And it all stemmed from one rule she lived by: **do good business.**

She paid vendors on time. She showed up early. She didn't cut corners. She never took money under the table. And when she made a mistake—because everyone does—she owned it before the client even noticed.

Word spread.

In a space full of shortcuts, Keisha stood out by simply being solid.

When the pandemic hit, many of her peers panicked. Cancelled events meant cancelled checks. But Keisha had options. Because of her reputation, clients trusted her with **non-refundable deposits**, knowing she'd reschedule or deliver value in another form. Vendors gave her extended payment terms. A former client, now working in tech, offered her a part-time remote marketing job—**just to help her stay afloat**.

"Don't think I forgot how you saved my wedding with that last-minute cake," he laughed on the Zoom call.

Reputation, she realized, had turned into **currency**.

As things bounced back, Keisha pivoted to digital event kits, consultation packages, and even launched a course on how to build client trust. Passive income. Affiliate deals. Brand partnerships. All of it possible not because she had the most followers—but because she had the most respect.

She once told a new mentee, "You don't have to sell cheap to get clients. Just be consistent, be clear, and be real. Trust builds repeat business. And repeat business builds empires."

That mentee? Booked out for months now. Thanks to Keisha's advice—and her referral.

Moral of the Story:
Reputation is currency. Branding isn't just your image—it's your integrity, your reliability, your ability to keep your word. In business and

in life, doing good business *is* good for business. The wealthiest people aren't always the flashiest—they're often the most trusted. Guard your name like an asset, because it is one.

Real-World Instructional: Reputation Is Branding. Branding Is Money.

Your **brand** isn't just your logo, color scheme, or IG grid.

Your **brand** is your name in the group chat when someone says, "Who do you know that can do this *right*?"

Keisha didn't out-market her competitors—she **out-reputed** them.

Here's how to build a reputation that keeps your name in rooms you haven't even walked into yet:

⭐ 1. Show Up on Time & Do What You Say

- Be early. Be consistent. Be dependable.
- If you're gonna be late or something changes—communicate clearly.
- Flaky people might still get clients. **But they rarely keep them.**

💬 2. Handle People Like They're Watching (Because They Are)

- Word of mouth spreads faster than hashtags.
- The way you treat **vendors**, **assistants**, **customers**, and **followers**—that's your brand.
- Kindness, professionalism, and a little humility go a long way.

💸 3. Honor Every Dollar Spent With You

- Whether a client spends $50 or $5,000, treat their money with the same care.

- People don't just remember your work—they remember **how they felt doing business with you**.

🧹 4. Clean Up Your Digital House

- If someone Googles your name, what shows up?
- Are your profiles consistent? Is your contact info easy to find?
- Pro Tip: Keep personal drama and professional pages separate.

🔁 5. The Best Clients Come From Repeat Clients

- Follow up. Ask for testimonials. Send thank-you notes.
- People love to feel seen—and they love sending money to people they trust.

> Remember: **A good name is better than a quick sale.**
> You're not just building a brand—you're building **legacy leverage.**

🎯 Sidebar: Are You Protecting the Bag or Playing Yourself in Public?™

If You're Still...	Then You Might Be...
Arguing with clients in the comments	Throwing away money and future referrals 😬

Ghosting on deadlines or delivering late	Building a reputation as "that vendor" 👻
Changing prices mid-project with no heads-up	Creating chaos and confusion (and refund requests) 😅
Posting more drama than product	Turning your timeline into a warning sign 🚩
"Rebranding" every 2 weeks because you're bored	Confusing your audience *and* your business identity 🌀
Forgetting that your name opens (or closes) doors	Leaving real money on the table 😐

Moral?
Reputation is like seasoning—once it's off, **nobody wants the rest of the dish.**

Book 8:

Debt Trap vs. Credit Mastery

Jordan posted a photo of her latest flip—fresh paint, clean staging, sleek kitchen. The caption read:
"Bought with business credit. Flipped in 3 months. $47K profit. Good credit = good leverage. Let's work."

She wasn't showing off—just documenting. That was her lane. Fix and flips. Smart renovations. Leveraging credit to build cash flow.

A few neighborhoods away, **Taj** sat in his car scrolling. His heart dropped a little as he stared at her post.

He had credit, too. Except his was maxed out across five cards. $22,000 in debt, mostly from trying to "invest in himself" without a real plan—courses he didn't finish, clothes he couldn't afford, and a failed vending machine business he never placed. Interest was eating him alive. Minimum payments. No progress. His phone buzzed with daily reminders and overdue notices.

But he remembered Jordan. They went to high school together. She wasn't flashy. Never had been. Just consistent. Lowkey.

He DM'd her:
Taj: "Yo, I saw your post. How did you even start flipping houses? I wanna get outta this hole."
Jordan: "You got time to hop on a call tomorrow?"
Taj: "Bet."

The next day, Jordan didn't sugarcoat anything.

"You don't have a money problem," she told him. "You have a **strategy problem**. Credit is a tool. You just been using it like it's candy."

Taj laughed nervously. "It felt good when I had access to it. Now I feel like it owns me."

"I get it," she said. "But I flipped my first property using **business credit**—$30K from a 0% interest card. I bought smart, stayed under budget, sold quick, and paid it off before the promo ended."

Taj shook his head. "See… that's wild. I've never thought of credit like that."

"That's the difference," she said. "One of us is letting it **work**, and one of us is working for it."

She told him about a **real estate funding course** that changed everything for her—how to get LLC funding, how to pitch a flip deal to a lender, how to structure a rehab budget. It cost **$497**.

"$497?" Taj blinked. "I'm already drowning in debt."

"And you'll stay there," Jordan said bluntly, "if you keep looking at money like a risk and not a resource."

"Scared money don't make none," she added. "You've got to bet on your **discipline**, not just your desire."

Taj hesitated. But after two days, a check-in message from Jordan, and a look at his statement balances, he paid for the course—with the last of his available credit.

Six months later, Taj had cleaned up one card, started budgeting properly, and used his tax refund to fund a small cosmetic flip with Jordan's help. He split profits, paid off more debt, and was finally learning to move **strategically**, not emotionally.

He wasn't rich. Not yet. But he was in control now. And that changed everything.

Moral of the Story:
Credit can either build your life or bury it. It's not about the limit—it's about how you **leverage** it. Taj learned the hard way that debt without direction is a trap. Jordan showed him that when used right, credit is a key—not a cage.
Scared money don't make none—but smart money doesn't move without a plan.

Real-World Instructional: Credit Is a Tool—Not a Trap

There are two ways to use credit:

1. **Swipe-now-worry-later energy** (aka Taj's old life)
2. **Strategic leverage for wealth-building** (aka Jordan's blueprint)

Here's how to flip the script and make credit work for *you*:

📉 1. Stop Digging the Hole

- Know your numbers: Total debt, interest rates, minimum payments.
- Choose a method:
  - **Snowball**: Pay off the smallest card first.
  - **Avalanche**: Pay off the highest interest first.
- Cut unnecessary subscriptions. Cancel the "free trials" you forgot. Brew your coffee at home. (Yeah, we said it.)

📈 2. Build Your Credit the Smart Way

- Pay on time. Every time. Set calendar reminders or auto-pay.
- Keep utilization **below 30%** (ideally under 10%).
- Don't close old cards—they help your credit age.
- Check your credit report *at least* once a year (for free).

🏗 3. Use Credit as Leverage, Not a Crutch

- Start an **LLC** and open a **business credit card**.
- Use 0% intro APR cards to fund cash-flowing projects **with a plan**.
- Never swipe just because you can—**swipe with strategy.**

📚 4. Invest in What You Can Apply

- Courses, coaching, mentorships—only if you're gonna **do the work**.
- Taj didn't just *buy* the course—he **studied it, used it, and profited from it.**

💡 5. Mindset Over Limit

- It's not about how much credit you can get—it's about how smart you are with it.
- Credit is like fire: It can cook your dinner or burn your house down. **Learn to control the flame.**

> **Pro Tip:** Real bosses use credit to make money—not to *look* like they have it.

😂 Sidebar: Are You Leveraging Credit or Getting Whooped by It?™

If You're Still...	Then You're Probably...
Swiping your card to "feel better"	Paying interest on your mood swings 😭
Opening store cards for the 10% discount	Getting 20% back in regret every month 💳💔
Bragging about your limit, not your usage rate	Flexing yourself into financial frustration 🥴
Paying the minimum like it's a flex	Taking 30 years to pay off brunch 💸📉
Ignoring your statements until they scream	Letting your mail carry more drama than TV shows 📬📺

Hesitating to invest in learning, but buying shoes fast	Styling your way into another cycle 👟➡️📉

Lesson?

You can either **pay interest** or **earn from your intelligence.**

Scared money stays broke. Strategic money builds freedom.

Book 9:

Protection Is a Wealth Strategy

Ashur Jamison was one of the hardest-working men you'd meet. He ran a mobile detailing business on the west side, and he didn't mind the long days or dirty work. He liked being in control of his time, his money, and his name. Clients loved him. His truck was always clean, his hands always busy. He was raising his younger brother, Micah, after their mom passed away, and as far as he was concerned, as long as he kept working, they'd be okay.

But what Ashur didn't see coming was how quickly life could flip the script—and how unprepared he really was.

It happened on a Tuesday. Micah had been riding his motorcycle home from class when a truck clipped him switching lanes. Ashur got the call while wiping down the hood of a Chevy Tahoe. The voice on the phone was calm and clinical. ICU. Emergency surgery. No insurance.

Ashur dropped everything.

The hospital smelled like bleach and anxiety. Doctors explained the situation, but all Ashur heard was paralysis, multiple surgeries, rehab, long recovery. Micah was alive, but broken. Ashur was stunned. Then the bills came.

Ambulance transport. Thousands. ICU stay. Six grand per day. Surgery. Medication. Machines Ashur couldn't pronounce. The numbers were wild, and none of it was covered. He had no emergency fund, no health coverage, no long-term care plan—just a few thousand in the bank and a couple credit cards that maxed out in a week.

He stopped working. Slept in a chair at the hospital. Ignored client calls. He begged for extensions, borrowed from friends, tried GoFundMe. But it wasn't enough. And every day, Micah needed more.

That's when Kehlani showed up.

They'd grown up on the same block. She was the type who always knew where her papers were and never missed a payment. Ashur used to clown her for being uptight. Now, he watched her walk into the hospital with a box of snacks and a folder under her arm like she was on a mission.

"I'm not here to sell you anything," she said, pulling up a chair. "I've been here. Not the accident, but the chaos. My mom had a stroke last year. But we planned. She had long-term care insurance. A living trust. A healthcare directive. Her house was in a trust, so I didn't have to deal with probate. I had power of attorney and access to funds. It was hard emotionally—but not financially. I want that for you."

Ashur stared at her, exhausted. "I didn't think I needed all that. I thought if I just worked hard, everything else would work itself out."

"That's the lie they sell us," she said gently. "That hustle is enough. But hustle without protection is a gamble."

Kehlani stayed in touch. She showed him her policies, explained how living benefits on life insurance worked, and how she'd used a Roth IRA to take time off work without panicking. She talked him through the basics of emergency funds, durable power of attorney, and the importance of having assets organized through a trust—not just to save taxes, but to save time and trauma.

When Micah was stable enough to go home, Ashur had nothing left. Not in his bank account. Not in his body. Not in his mind. But what he did have now was awareness—and a plan to rebuild.

He picked up extra shifts. Sold old equipment. Cut subscriptions, created a new budget, and started small. He opened a high-yield savings account and began building a three-month emergency fund. He bought a term life insurance policy with living benefits, opened a Roth IRA, and made Kehlani his backup healthcare proxy. He set up a trust for Micah and added a long-term care rider to his insurance in case life threw another curveball.

He also started thinking about retirement. Not as a dream, but as a number. He didn't want to be sixty-five and still climbing ladders with wax buckets. Kehlani explained how retirement wasn't just about age—it was about building enough cash flow to live with dignity. She helped him create a plan with a mix of Roth contributions, investment accounts, and eventually a solo 401(k) once he restructured his business as an S-Corp.

Ashur no longer wanted to work forever. He wanted to work **smart**—then rest **well**.

A year later, Micah was walking again, slowly. Ashur's business was thriving. Clients came back. New clients referred others. And Ashur? He became the man in the barbershop talking about insurance like it was a flex.

"You got health insurance?" he'd ask someone in the waiting chair. "Nah? Better fix that. I almost went broke thinking nothing bad could happen."

He laughed sometimes when he caught himself sounding like Kehlani. She, on the other hand, had become the go-to in the community for all things planning. She didn't brag, she just helped. Quietly. Intentionally. Efficiently. And when a group of financially free minds came together in the final chapter to build something bigger than themselves, Kehlani had a seat at the table.

Because real wealth isn't just about what you make—it's about what you protect. And preparation? That's peace you can't put a price on.

Moral of the Story:
You can't prevent every emergency. But you can prevent it from becoming a **financial disaster.**
Long-term care insurance, emergency funds, life insurance, trusts, and retirement planning don't mean you expect bad things—they mean you're building a **plan that protects your peace**, your people, and your progress.
Because wealth isn't just what you build.
It's what you keep—and what you prepare for.

Real-World Instructional: If You Love It—Protect It

Here's the truth most people learn the hard way:
Emergencies don't ask if you're ready. They just arrive.

Ashur didn't fail because he didn't care—he failed because he didn't prepare. Here's how to make sure you're not next.

Build an Emergency Fund

- Start small: aim for **$1,000**, then build up to **3–6 months of expenses**.
- Keep it **liquid and accessible**, like in a **high-yield savings account**.
- Emergency funds aren't just for car trouble—they're for **life trouble**.

Get Life Insurance (Yes, Even If You're Young)

- **Term life** is affordable and protects your loved ones if something happens.
- Add **living benefits** (critical illness, chronic care) so you can access funds while alive if needed.
- Don't wait until you "have money"—you get it **so they do**.

Plan for Long-Term Care

- 70% of people over 65 will need it. Most insurance **doesn't cover it**.
- LTC insurance helps pay for in-home care, rehab, assisted living, etc.
- If you wait too long, you may become **uninsurable**.

Establish a Trust and Will

- Avoid probate court delays and fees.
- Keep assets protected and directed *exactly* where you want them.

- Include **durable power of attorney** and **healthcare directives** so your family isn't left guessing.

🧓 Start Retirement Now—Not Later

- Even **$100/month** in a **Roth IRA** makes a massive difference over time.
- You want options, not overtime, when you hit 60.
- Retirement is not a dream. **It's a deadline.**

> **"Protection planning isn't about expecting the worst—it's about respecting the life you've built."**

🤕 Sidebar: Are You Built for Storms—or Just Hoping It Doesn't Rain?™

If You're Still Saying...	You Might Be...
"I'll get insurance later, I'm healthy right now."	One fall away from GoFundMe 😬
"My job has benefits, that's enough."	Under-protected and over-confident 😅
"Trusts are for rich people."	About to let probate eat your legacy 💸

"I'll worry about retirement when I'm older."	Stuck working forever with creaky knees 🦵💼
"I've got a little saved, I'll be fine."	One ER bill away from overdraft 🚑📉
"If something happens, I'll figure it out."	Already behind. Life doesn't wait. 🕒

Take?
Protection isn't paranoia—it's power.
Plan ahead so your future doesn't come crashing down later.

Book 10:

Health Is Wealth

CJ Jacobs was a machine. At least, that's what everyone called him.

He was the kind of person who'd outwork anybody in the room. Early mornings. Late nights. No breaks. No sick days. No slowing down. He took pride in it. While other people were sleeping in or calling out, CJ Jacobs was on his grind—clocking into his job, running his side hustle, and plotting his investments on the side.

He didn't eat right, but he made deposits. He didn't sleep much, but he paid bills on time. And even though his back ached and his chest felt tight more days than not, he'd say, "I'll rest when I'm rich."

Except, that rest came sooner than expected—and not the way he imagined.

It started with fatigue he couldn't shake. Then headaches. Shortness of breath. The stress finally caught up to him when he collapsed at work and woke up in the ER.
Blood pressure through the roof. Elevated cholesterol. Pre-diabetic. Severe inflammation. And exhaustion that had been building for years.

"You're lucky," the doctor told him. "This could've been worse. But it's time to slow down—permanently."

CJ Jacobs couldn't believe it. He was 38. Strong. Built. Respected.
But inside? He was breaking down.

The truth was, CJ Jacobs had been sacrificing his health chasing money—when really, he'd need his health to enjoy it later.

The next few weeks were sobering.

Doctors' appointments replaced meetings. Prescriptions replaced paychecks. He had to take medical leave from work. His hustle stopped cold. And for the first time in a decade, CJ Jacobs had to ask for help.

It was Kehlani—the financial advisor who had once helped Ashur—who stepped in.

"I see this all the time," she told him. "People who work themselves sick. Stack the paper, but lose the body."

CJ Jacobs looked at her, frustrated. "What's the point of building wealth if I can't even enjoy it?"

"Exactly," she said. "Health *is* wealth. Don't just invest in your future bank account—invest in your future *self.*"

CJ Jacobs started over. This time, slowly.

He changed his diet. Went for walks. Slept 8 hours. Took time off when needed. Saw a therapist. And with Kehlani's help, he restructured his finances to give himself breathing room. He created a health savings account (HSA), increased his insurance coverage, and started investing in longevity—not just income.

He sold one of his rental properties to take the financial pressure off, and used the proceeds to build passive income that didn't require physical labor.

Over time, he felt different. Lighter. Clearer. Richer in ways that didn't show up on a balance sheet.

He started mentoring young guys in his neighborhood about balancing ambition with wellness. "The grind will always be there," he told them. "But your body? Your peace? You only get one of those."

CJ Jacobs still had goals. He still wanted wealth. But now, he knew the real flex wasn't burning out to get there—it was making it there with his health intact.

Moral of the Story:
You can earn all the money in the world, but it means nothing if you lose

your health along the way. CJ Jacobs learned that longevity matters more than lifestyle. Health isn't a luxury—it's a requirement for freedom. True wealth is being able to enjoy your money with a sound mind, strong body, and peaceful heart.

Real-World Instructional: Build the Bag Without Breaking Your Body

Let's keep it real:
Grinding 24/7 without rest is not a flex—it's a fast-track to burnout.

CJ Jacobs learned the hard way that health isn't optional. It's the *foundation* for everything you're building.

Here's how to protect your health *while* pursuing wealth:

🥦 1. Eat Like You Love Yourself

- **You don't need a private chef to make smart food choices.**
- **Start small: cut down sugar, increase water, eat more whole foods.**
- **Avoid living off energy drinks and vending machine diets.**
  That's not hustle. That's slow self-destruction.

🛌 2. Rest is Productive

- **Sleep fuels focus, immunity, and decision-making.**
- **7–8 hours isn't lazy—it's longevity.**
- **"I'll sleep when I'm rich" is how you end up in the ER before 40.**

🧠 3. Protect Your Peace

- **Chronic stress increases the risk of heart disease, diabetes, and anxiety.**
- **Incorporate *mental hygiene*—therapy, meditation, walks, journaling.**
- **Set boundaries. Say "no." Every opportunity isn't worth your sanity.**

🧾 **4. Financial Health = Physical Health**

- **Money stress causes real health problems.**
- **Create breathing room with:**
    - **Emergency Fund**
    - **Health Savings Account (HSA)**
    - **Affordable Insurance (Health, Life, Disability)**
- **Don't wait for disaster to protect your body or your bank account.**

🌞 **5. Play the Long Game**

- **Prioritize sustainable income, not just fast money.**
- **Passive income and low-effort cash flow are the goal.**
- **A six-figure month doesn't mean much if you're too sick to enjoy it.**

> ***"Your body is the first business you ever owned—treat it like it pays your bills."***

😅 Sidebar: Are You Getting the Bag or Just Getting Beat Up By It?™

If You're Still...	Then You Might Be...
Working 16-hour days, 7 days a week	**Getting rich while falling apart inside 💼😵‍💫**

Eating like your stomach has a savings account	**Budgeting your way into blood pressure meds** 🩺🍟
Sleeping 4 hours and calling it discipline	**Practicing slow self-sabotage with a strong work ethic** 🛌😮‍💨
Pushing through headaches and chest pain	**Mistaking survival mode for success** 🚨
Skipping doctor visits to "save money"	**Setting up a $30,000 medical emergency fund the hard way** 💳🚑
Saying "I'll sleep when I'm rich"	**Sleeping in an ER bed when your body taps out** 😴🏥

Lesson?
The real boss move is to be healthy *and* wealthy.
Because if you're too sick to spend it, you never really had it.

Book 11:

Becoming Your Own Bank – The Power of Life Insurance

Marcus and Kevin grew up on the same block. Same schools, same hustle, same hunger. By the time they hit their twenties, both had jobs, ambition, and a vision for financial success. But the routes they took couldn't have been more different.

Marcus played it safe. He believed in working hard, stacking cash in a traditional savings account, maxing out his 401(k), and investing in stocks. He saw life insurance as something you only needed if you had kids or a mortgage.

Kevin, on the other hand, had learned something different—something most people never get taught. He studied how the wealthy use whole life insurance policies as powerful financial tools. Not just for death benefits, but for building wealth *while you're still alive.*

While Marcus saved and invested the traditional way, Kevin structured his money into a properly designed whole life insurance policy—the kind that built cash value over time. He treated it like his own private bank.

By the time they were forty, Marcus had saved around $50,000. His 401(k) was steady, but he always felt like he was behind. Anytime life hit him with an emergency or an opportunity, he had to either take on debt or withdraw from his savings—losing growth in the process.

Kevin's cash value had quietly grown to over $200,000 inside his policy. And he could borrow against it at any time—tax-free, penalty-free, no questions asked. The best part? His full policy value still earned interest *as if the money had never left.*

When a real estate deal popped up—a distressed triplex in a booming area—both wanted in.

Marcus applied for a traditional bank loan. Credit checks, paperwork, waiting games, and a not-so-friendly interest rate.

Kevin? He made one call, borrowed from his policy, closed on the deal, and started renovations the same week. He owed no one but himself. And when he paid back the loan—with interest—that interest went back into his own policy, not the bank's.

Over time, Kevin used the same strategy to fund other investments:
A used car lot. A commercial vending contract. His daughter's college tuition. Even medical expenses during a rough patch.
All without draining his savings or begging a bank for anything.

Marcus, meanwhile, hit a rough stretch during a recession. His investments dipped. His job cut hours. He needed cash fast—but everything was tied up or dropping in value. The banks weren't lending, and his savings barely earned enough to notice.

Over coffee one afternoon, Marcus leaned in and asked, "Man... how do you always seem to have access to money, no matter what's going on?"

Kevin smiled and stirred his tea. "I stopped letting banks control my cash flow. I became my own bank."

Marcus sat back, quiet. It wasn't flashy. It wasn't magic. It was discipline, structure, and a strategy most people never hear about.

Kevin explained the truth behind how the wealthy really use life insurance:

- Cash Value Growth: His whole life policy grew *guaranteed*, tax-deferred, every year—regardless of market swings.
- Living Benefits: He could access funds during his lifetime—no waiting for death to see value.
- Tax-Free Loans: He could borrow without penalties, keep his money growing, and pay himself back with interest.
- Legacy Protection: If anything happened to him, his family would receive a tax-free payout, instantly transferring wealth.
- Control Over Capital: No bank approvals. No credit checks. No waiting games.

Most people don't realize that life insurance is the only investment that's guaranteed. No volatility. No crash risk. Just consistency, security, and leverage.

Marcus finally understood. Working hard was good. Saving was responsible. But leverage and liquidity were the missing pieces. Becoming your own banker wasn't just a hack—it was the foundation of real financial freedom.

Moral of the Story:
Life insurance isn't just about what happens when you die—it's about how you live. It's a tool that offers cash value, tax-free growth, and unmatched control. When you become your own bank, you stop asking for permission to use your own money—and start building wealth on your own terms. Because the best investor isn't just smart—it's protected, prepared, and in control.

Real-World Instructional: Become Your Own Bank—For Real

Most people have no idea that properly structured life insurance can be used like a personal bank.
Not for "when you die," but to build wealth while you're alive.

Here's how Bryce did it—and how you can too:

🏦 1. Choose the Right Type of Policy

- **Not all life insurance is created equal.**
- **You need a whole life or indexed universal life (IUL) policy designed for cash value, not just the death benefit.**
- **Work with a licensed agent who specializes in infinite banking or wealth-building strategies—not a cookie-cutter rep.**

💰 2. Fund It Intentionally

- **This isn't a "pay the bare minimum" setup. You fund it like a bank account.**
- **The more you contribute early, the faster your cash value grows.**
- **The money grows tax-deferred and earns guaranteed interest (plus potential dividends depending on the carrier).**

🔁 3. Borrow from Yourself

- **Once your cash value grows, you can take loans against it at any time.**
- **No credit check. No approval. No penalty.**
- **Your policy continues to grow as if the money was never withdrawn.**
- **Repay the loan on your own terms—and when you do, the interest goes back to you, not the bank.**

🛡️ 4. Get Living & Death Benefits

- If something happens to you, your family gets a tax-free lump sum payout.
- Many policies come with living benefits: access to funds in the case of illness, injury, or long-term care needs.
- You're not just investing—you're protecting your legacy at the same time.

📈 5. Use It for Wealth Moves

Use your policy to:

- Fund real estate deals
- Pay for college
- Cover emergencies
- Launch a business
- Replace retirement income

You don't have to *lose* money to use it—your money works twice: once in your policy, and again wherever you reinvest it.

> **"The bank makes money off your money. Why not do the same—for yourself?"**

😎 Sidebar: Are You the Bank or Just Another Broke Depositor?™

If You're Still Saying...	Then You Might Be...

"Life insurance is just for death."	**Missing out on the wealth game while breathing 💨**
"I'll use my savings if something comes up."	**Earning 0.02% while inflation eats your lunch 🥴**
"I'd rather borrow from a real bank."	**Paying strangers to use your own potential 💸**
"I can't afford that kind of policy."	**But can afford DoorDash four times a week 😅**
"It sounds too good to be true."	**But your broke cousin is your emergency fund 🤐**
"I'll worry about insurance when I'm older."	**Plot twist: You'll pay more, get less, and regret it 🌚😬**

Lesson?
Be like Bryce. Build the bank. Become the bank.
Charlique had discipline. But Bryce had control.

Book 12 - The Final Chapter:

The Circle – From Lessons to Legacy

It started with a group text.

Sophia sent it out first.
"Been thinking… what if we didn't just learn about money separately—what if we built something together?"

One by one, the responses poured in.

Giorgi was in. He had already scaled back his spending and was ready to invest with purpose.
Wolf replied next, fresh off a partnership expansion with Tami and ready to diversify.
Bryce, the life insurance strategist, offered to host.
Kehlani, always organized, offered to bring the folders.
Ashur, now debt-free and finally breathing easy, brought the snacks—and the spreadsheets.
CJ Jacobs, healthy and focused, volunteered to lead the fitness breaks.
Sophia invited her old investor circle: Tanya and Joyner, both eager to make smarter, more strategic moves now.
Jordan, who built her hair brand from nothing, showed up with her son's NFL connections and an idea for a mentorship nonprofit.
Leon Wills Jr., poised and humble, brought real estate blueprints, income reports, and the wisdom of his late father.
And Charlique, eyes wide, took notes—this time ready to listen, learn, and finally shift from discipline to ownership.

They met at a coworking space owned by one of Bryce's clients. Long table. Whiteboard. Pitch deck playing on a mounted TV.

This wasn't just a "talk about money" meetup.
This was the beginning of something real.

"I've been thinking a lot about assets," Sophia said. "Passive income, yes—but also ownership. Real ownership. Businesses, real estate, intellectual property."

Leon nodded. "Assets and systems. We inherited income-producing properties. What's missing is organized collaboration."

"We could start a firm," Giorgi said, leaning forward. "One that brings together our different strengths—consulting, real estate, brand strategy, funding."

Kehlani raised a hand. "And structure it legally. Trusts. Tax planning. That way, this isn't just a moment. It's a movement."

Wolf looked around. "We already have the pieces. We just haven't put them together yet."

CJ laughed. "We really gonna be *that* group?"

"No," Bryce said. "We're gonna be better."

They began mapping it out.

- A joint venture fund.
- An investment club.
- A digital learning platform.
- A community scholarship backed by their earnings.
- Business funding programs for young entrepreneurs.

But more than that—they built trust.

The circle wasn't about who made the most or looked the richest.
It was about shared wisdom, real transparency, and collective legacy.

They didn't agree on everything. Some wanted to move faster. Others, more cautious. But every voice had value. Every seat at the table was earned.

By the end of the meeting, they had a name.
The Wealth Circle.

A mission: to build, protect, and pass on wealth—together.

And a promise:
To never gatekeep knowledge.
To invest with purpose.
To teach the next generation what they never got taught.

As they locked in hands at the end of the meeting, no one said much. But everyone knew:

This wasn't the end of the journey. It was just the beginning.

Moral of the Story:
The richest thing you can build is community.
Legacy isn't just what you leave behind—it's what you build *with others* in the present.
When minds align, wealth multiplies.
Collaboration is the ultimate currency.

Closing Message

You made it to the end—and in doing so, you've joined a growing number of people who are waking up to a truth that was never meant to stay hidden:

Wealth is not just about money. It's about choices, control, and legacy.

The characters in this book represent real people. Real stories. Real decisions that change lives—not overnight, but over time.

Some started with very little. Others earned a lot and nearly lost it. Some were late to the game, while others built quietly behind the scenes. But they all share something in common:
They took the lessons, faced the truth, and made the shift—from working for money to letting money work for them.

And now, it's your turn.

Budget smarter.
Invest with intention.
Protect your peace and your people.
Start the business. Read the policy. Fund the trust.
Ask the questions. Do the research. Break the cycle.

Whether you're just starting out or already deep in your financial journey, know this:

> **You don't have to be perfect to build wealth—you just have to be consistent.**

And when you're ready… build your own circle.
Because legacy doesn't end with you—it begins because of you.

The blueprint is in your hands now. Build your legacy.

Author's Note

My name is Lahsann C. Rogers, and like many of the stories in this book, my journey to financial literacy wasn't linear—and it definitely wasn't easy.

I passed my Series 7, Series 63, and Series 10-55. I earned my real estate license. I studied business in college. I even incorporated my first company back in 2004 at just 17 years old. And I spent a stretch of time working on Wall Street, chasing dreams and absorbing the language of money at its most intense level.

Some of my coworkers were making $300,000 a month. And yet… I didn't have the same success. There were times when my own income was so low, I didn't know if I'd see the next day—financially or mentally. I battled fear, uncertainty, and the pressure to keep up. I failed. I started over. And then I kept going.

What I had was my health, my mind, and an unshakable belief that I could rebuild. So I did.

I learned how to use everything I knew—from securities and investing, to budgeting and real estate—and I applied it not just to portfolios, but to life. I realized that financial freedom wasn't about how much you make. It's about what you keep, how you use it, and how you grow it over time.

This book is for the grinders. The quiet savers. The single parents. The tired hustlers. The paycheck-to-paycheck survivors. The people who never got taught—but never gave up.

I wrote this because I lived it.
And if I could make it out with the cards I was dealt—so can you.

Let this book be your blueprint, your reminder, and your push to build something real.

Because the freedom you're looking for isn't in a paycheck.
It's in the way you move. The way you plan. The way you believe.

Let's build.

—

Lahsann C. Rogers
Entrepreneur | Investor | Educator | Survivor

Acknowledgments

First and always, I give thanks to God—for the wisdom, provision, and strength to keep going when everything in me wanted to quit. Every chapter I lived through, every lesson I've learned, and every page in this book is only possible because of His grace. He carried me when I didn't know how to carry myself.

To those who understand the lessons in this book—who feel the truth of each story in your bones—this is for you. If you're budgeting with intention, building with limited resources, or trying to change the financial future for your family... stay the course.

Don't give up.
Don't compare yourself to others.
Look inward. Stay focused.
Keep moving forward—not backward.

To those who are close, on the edge of change, hungry to learn but unsure how—don't stop. There is power in humility, power in asking, and power in discipline. Everything you need is already within you.

To the eager learners, the late bloomers, the comeback stories, the quiet builders—this book is your blueprint, your confirmation, your reminder that you are not alone.

And to the names of the characters inspired by my family members—whether you saw yourselves in the story or not—know that I love you deeply. Your presence, your impact, and your legacy are written into these pages in ways that matter.

This book was birthed from real life, real struggle, and real hope. And I'm honored that you're holding it in your hands.

Thank you for believing in something better. Let's build forward—together.

—

Lahsann C. Rogers

Summary of Books & Morals

Book 1- The Cost of Living vs. The Price of Freedom

Giorgi earns a high salary as a corporate attorney but lives paycheck to paycheck due to overspending and lifestyle inflation. After a wake-up call from his firm, he reevaluates his finances, pays off debt, starts investing, and learns that true wealth is built by keeping and growing what you earn.

- ☐ **Moral: It's not about how much you make—it's about how much you keep, invest, and let work for you.**

Book 2 - Money Isn't Everything—The Way We Use It Is

Three friends invest in the same portfolio but take different approaches: one times the market, one chases the highs, and one invests consistently no matter what. Over 20 years, it's Sophia—the consistent investor—who builds the most wealth through compound interest and discipline.

- ☐ **Moral: Wealth favors consistency—invest regularly, stay the course, and let time do the heavy lifting.**

Book 3: - The Language of Money

Giorgi is offered partnership at his law firm but chooses to build his own. With guidance from a banker and a savvy entrepreneur, he learns how to use business structure, debt, and tax strategy to his advantage. By speaking the language of money and stepping into ownership, he transforms his career and income.

- ☐ **Moral: Ownership speaks the language of wealth—learn it, use it, and build freedom.**

Book 4: Why Saving & Investing Matter More Than Spending

Mr. Leon Wills, a humble school janitor, lived a quiet life of discipline and intentionality—never spending above his means, avoiding debt, and investing in bonds, stocks, and real estate. When he passed, he left behind a $10 million legacy through trusts, assets, and cash flow. His story proves that wealth isn't built in the spotlight—it's built in silence.

- ☐ **Moral: You don't have to look rich to be wealthy—save smart, invest wisely, and let time do the heavy lifting.**

Book 5: The Power of Budgeting & Avoiding Debt

Tasha, a single mother working two jobs and running a side hustle, used budgeting to survive and build a path to financial freedom. By managing debt, living below her means, and staying laser-focused, she not only grew her hair business—but taught her NFL-bound son how to handle wealth with wisdom.

- ☐ **Moral: Budgeting isn't a burden—it's a blueprint for freedom. Even with limited income, discipline and strategy can change your entire legacy.**

Book 6: Entrepreneurship, Partnerships & Passive Income

Wolf had a skill. His brother Zeke didn't see the vision, but his friend Tami did—and together, they built a mobile tech repair business from scratch. When Zeke came around, he joined the team and helped scale the company. With passive income streams and solid systems, they turned a side hustle into a thriving enterprise.

☐ **Moral: Ownership builds wealth, partnerships multiply it, and when the vision is clear—family, friends, and passive income all have a seat at the table.**

Book 7: Your Reputation Is a Financial Asset

Keisha built her brand through consistency, professionalism, and integrity—not flashy marketing. When challenges hit, her reputation opened doors, created new income streams, and earned long-term trust from clients. Her story proves that doing good business is one of the smartest financial moves you can make.

☐ **Moral: Reputation is a form of currency. Protect your name, honor your word, and let integrity be your brand—it will open doors money alone never could.**

Book 8: Debt Trap vs. Credit Mastery

Taj found himself buried in credit card debt while Jordan was using her credit to fund profitable real estate flips. After seeing her success, he reached out, took a chance on learning, and began his journey toward using credit strategically instead of emotionally. With mentorship and mindset, he turned his credit story around.

☐ **Moral: Credit isn't the enemy—misuse is. When managed wisely, credit becomes a tool for wealth. Scared money stays stuck, but smart money builds freedom.**

Book 9: Protection Is a Wealth Strategy

Ashur never thought about insurance or long-term planning—until a family emergency nearly destroyed everything he'd built. With guidance from Kehlani, he learned the importance of life insurance, trusts, long-term care, emergency funds, and retirement planning. That protection didn't just save him from disaster—it gave him peace of mind.

- ☐ **Moral: Hustle builds income. Preparation protects it. Wealth isn't just about growth—it's about being ready when life happens.**

Book 10: Health Is Wealth

CJ worked non stop chasing success, ignoring the warning signs from his body until a health crisis forced him to stop. With support and financial restructuring, he learned to prioritize rest, nutrition, and peace—realizing that no amount of money is worth your health. Wealth means nothing if you're too sick to enjoy it.

- ☐ **Moral: Health isn't a luxury—it's the foundation of freedom. Protect your body the same way you protect your money, because true wealth means being alive, well, and able to enjoy what you've built.**

Book 11: Becoming Your Own Bank – The Power of Life Insurance

Charlique followed the traditional financial route—save, invest, borrow from the bank. Bryce took a different path, using a properly structured whole life insurance policy to build wealth, access cash, and fund his investments on his own terms. While Charlique struggled with restrictions, Bryce leveraged his policy like a personal bank—building freedom, not just savings.

- ☐ **Moral: Life insurance isn't just protection—it's a wealth-building tool. When you become your own bank, you don't just secure your future—you control it.**

Book 12 - The Final Chapter: The Circle – From Lessons to Legacy

All the main characters come together, each bringing their financial lessons, experiences, and strengths. From budgeting and investing to real estate, business, insurance, and protection—they form a collective called The Wealth Circle. Together, they commit to building, protecting, and passing on generational wealth through collaboration and intentional strategy.

- ☐ **Moral: Legacy isn't built alone. True wealth multiplies through unity, trust, and shared purpose. Collaboration is the ultimate financial power move.**

Apply the Blueprint: Reflective Questions.

Lessons, Takeaways + Journal Prompts

Book 1: The Cost of Living vs. The Price of Freedom

Lesson: A high income doesn't guarantee financial stability—what matters is how you manage what you keep.
Takeaway: Spending to maintain appearances will quietly destroy your wealth. Budgeting and investing create real freedom.
Journal Prompts:

- Am I living above, below, or within my means?
- What expenses could I cut without lowering my quality of life?
- What does financial freedom actually look like for me—and am I moving toward it?

Book 2: Money Isn't Everything—The Way We Use It Is

Lesson: Consistency beats timing. The market rewards those who stay the course.
Takeaway: You don't need to be perfect—you just need to be disciplined. Time and compound interest will do the rest.
Journal Prompts:

- Am I investing regularly—even when it's uncomfortable?
- What's stopping me from automating my investments?
- How can I build habits that make investing second nature?

Book 3: The Language of Money

Lesson: Owning your time and income starts with learning how money moves—taxes, leverage, and structure matter.
Takeaway: Entrepreneurship isn't just about hustle—it's about understanding systems. That's where the freedom is.
Journal Prompts:

- Am I using my current job to build, or just to survive?
- Do I understand how taxes and debt can work in my favor?
- What would I build if I weren't afraid of failure—or of success?

Book 4: Why Saving & Investing Matter More Than Spending

Lesson: Wealth is built in the background, not the spotlight. Quiet discipline outlasts loud spending.
Takeaway: You don't have to earn millions to be wealthy. You need patience, strategy, and a plan.
Journal Prompts:

- Am I living beneath my means in a way that serves me?
- Where can I invest quietly and consistently?
- What legacy am I building—and for who?

Book 5: The Power of Budgeting & Avoiding Debt

Lesson: Budgeting isn't a burden—it's a tool for clarity and control.
Takeaway: You can build wealth on any income when your mindset, habits, and numbers align.
Journal Prompts:

- Do I have a written budget that reflects my goals?
- Where is my money going without my permission?
- What debt am I carrying that's holding me back?

Book 6: Entrepreneurship, Partnerships & Passive Income

Lesson: Your skillset can build wealth when matched with the right partners and systems.
Takeaway: Collaboration can multiply your results. Passive income begins with intentional planning.
Journal Prompts:

- What problem can I solve with my skillset?
- Who around me has what I'm missing—and how can we build together?

- Where in my life can I build income that doesn't depend on hours worked?

Book 7: Your Reputation Is a Financial Asset

Lesson: Reputation is currency. Integrity can be more valuable than capital.
Takeaway: People invest in people they trust. Do good business and your name will open doors.
Journal Prompts:

- What do people associate with my name or brand?
- Am I consistently delivering value and professionalism?
- Where do I need to clean up my digital or real-world presence?

Book 8: Debt Trap vs. Credit Mastery

Lesson: Credit can build you or break you—it all depends on how you use it.
Takeaway: The real power lies in using credit as a tool, not a trap.
Journal Prompts:

- Do I know my current credit score and debt situation?
- Am I borrowing emotionally or strategically?
- How can I use credit to invest in income-producing assets?

Book 9: Protection Is a Wealth Strategy

Lesson: Emergencies are inevitable. Preparation turns chaos into calm.
Takeaway: Insurance, emergency funds, and estate planning aren't optional—they're essential.
Journal Prompts:

- Do I have protections in place for myself and my family?
- What would happen financially if I got sick or couldn't work?
- What steps can I take today to protect my legacy?

Book 10: Health Is Wealth

Lesson: No amount of money matters if you don't have your health.
Takeaway: Wellness is the foundation of wealth. Prioritize it or risk losing everything you built.
Journal Prompts:

- Am I sacrificing my health in the name of success?
- How can I build rest, nutrition, and movement into my routine?
- What does a wealthy, *well* version of me look and feel like?

Book 11: Becoming Your Own Bank – The Power of Life Insurance

Lesson: You can leverage life insurance to build, borrow, and grow wealth—while alive.
Takeaway: The wealthiest people use properly structured policies to create tax-free income and financial freedom. So can you.
Journal Prompts:

- Do I understand the difference between term and whole life insurance?
- What would it mean to become my own bank?
- How can I use life insurance to create both protection and opportunity?

Book 12: The Circle – From Lessons to Legacy

Lesson: Wealth multiplies in community. Legacy is built together.
Takeaway: Collaboration, shared vision, and trust are the final keys to generational wealth.
Journal Prompts:

- Who do I need to build with—and what am I waiting for?
- How can I share my knowledge without gatekeeping?
- What legacy do I want to create, protect, and pass on—and who will carry it forward?

About the Author

Lahsann C. Rogers is a multifaceted entrepreneur, real estate professional, actor, and four-time published author. A native of New York, Lahsann brings a powerful blend of lived experience, business insight, and creative vision to every venture he touches.

He began his journey in the financial world, passing his Series 7, 63, and 10-55 licenses, and even working on Wall Street—where he witnessed firsthand the highs and lows of wealth-building. Despite being surrounded by brokers making over $300,000 a month, Lahsann faced moments when his own future was uncertain. Those experiences grounded him, shaped his philosophy, and taught him a lasting truth:

> **"It's not about how much you make—it's about how you move."**

Transitioning out of financial services, Lahsann leaned fully into real estate—earning his license and becoming one of the first ten agents at The Real Brokerage Inc., a publicly traded company founded by Tamir Poleg. He played a key role in its early growth and now stands as a shareholder among 25,000+ agents nationwide.

As a real estate investor and professional, Lahsann has helped countless clients achieve their property goals while building his own portfolio with purpose and vision.

Beyond business, Lahsann is a dedicated creative—a musician and actor with credits in *Nobody's Perfect* (2016), *Dope King*, and *Discretion TV Hollywood NY* (2017). Equipped with the tools and vision for filmmaking, he is now preparing to adapt his published works, including the beloved Bita Series and this finance book, into full film productions.

His mission is clear:
To make wealth understandable, accessible, and sustainable—for those who weren't born into it, but are determined to build it.

Follow his journey and connect on Instagram: @say_itaint_sold

Other Books By Lahsann Rogers

Won't You Eat My NABR? A Culinary Journey Through North America's Best Recipes

📖 Won't You Eat My NABR? North America's Best Recipes 🍽️

Discover the Flavors of North America—One Iconic Dish at a Time!

From the bustling food scenes of New York, Los Angeles, and New Orleans to the authentic flavors of Mexico, Canada, and the Deep South, Won't You Eat My NABR? North America's Best Recipes takes you on a delicious journey through the continent's most famous dishes.

This 78-page cookbook features 46 expertly curated recipes, highlighting the top regional specialties from North America's greatest food cities. Whether it's Chicago's deep-dish pizza, Seattle's cedar-plank salmon, Montreal's poutine, or Mexico City's street tacos, each recipe is a tribute to the rich culinary diversity of the continent.

But this cookbook isn't just about geography—it's also personal. Included are 8 special recipes that are near and dear to my heart, hand-picked from my own kitchen and my family's most cherished meals. While these may not all be from North America, they bring a unique and personal touch to this collection.

And because every great cook has their own signature dish, you'll find a blank new recipe page at the end—a special space for you to add your own favorite recipe to this book, making it truly your own.

Whether you're an adventurous home cook, a lover of regional cuisine, or someone looking to bring the taste of North America into your kitchen, this book is your guide to the best dishes from across the continent and into the Caribbean.

🔥 Explore. Cook. Savor. Won't You Eat My NABR?

📌 Perfect for:

✅ Food lovers and home cooks

✅ Fans of regional cuisine and travel-inspired cooking

✅ Anyone looking to expand their recipe collection with authentic North American classics

Order now and start your culinary journey today! 🍴🔥

My Learning WorkBook - Alphabet, Numbers, Animals and Shapes

✏️ Learn to draw the ABCs with this amazing coloring book for kids 3-5 years old! 👦

🎨 Work this workbook one activity page at a time! 🦁 Work books like this are a great way for children to learn. Not only will your kids have fun, but they'll engage with new lessons and get an education while playing! 😸

🔊 What's in this Kids Coloring Book:

▪ 150+ coloring pages for toddlers and children

▪ Large coloring area and thick lines. Numbers and shapes to trace, Animals, cars, alphabet, numbers and shapes skip counting, reflective symmetry and more

▪ Fun and child-friendly pictures to color

▪ Single sided designs with a variety of pictures

▪ Jumbo coloring pages for kids

✨ Fun Coloring Activities for Boys and Girls:

▪ Uppercase and lowercase alphabet coloring pages (from A to Z) Numbers from 1-100, different animals to color, number Line tracing, mathematics and reflection symmetry drawing

▪ Activities like coloring, find the odd one out, maze, and more.

▪ Dot to dot puzzles with colorable pages

▪ Pictures of sea and land animals to color in!

✔️ This is the perfect alphabet coloring book for children of all ages, toddlers to preschoolers, kindergarteners and up. 🔥 Not only will it help teach kids their ABCs, and numbers, and cognitive skills but they'll also improve their pencil control and boost color recognition skills. Best of all, they'll have fun while doing it and will progress with this book as they grow they can do some of the more difficult challenges like skip counting

🎓 Get this jumbo workbook today and help your child start their learning adventure! 🚀

ABC Alphabet, Animals, Shapes, Numbers and Line Coloring and Tracing workbook for toddlers, preschoolers, kindergarten children aged 1-8; daycare activities and learning Mathematics & skip counting

One Lucki Day - BITA Volume 1 -

Some days are lucky. Others change your life forever.

Lucki Prince Cunningbur was born in Texas — simple, smart, nerdy, corny, but deeply kind. Raised with heart and humility, he always carried his lucky rabbit's foot and treated people with care. Though he never sought the spotlight, his brilliance shined through. A gifted student and thoughtful soul, Lucki's path led him to the heights of corporate excellence: a coveted position at one of the world's most prestigious firms, Wilhemehna & Rodgers Company.

It's there he's given a career-defining task — to plan an exclusive gala for Jade Star.

Jade, an immigrant who rose from humble beginnings, conquered the world of entertainment through dance, song, and acting. With fame and fortune in abundance, she seemed untouchable — until she met Lucki. At the gala, their worlds collided. The chemistry was instant, the connection real.

But just as love begins to bloom, they're attacked by a member of the Beltrán Leyva cartel. They survive, but the scars run deep. Unbeknownst to Lucki, Jade's parents were murdered by the cartel years earlier. Their love, once full of promise, becomes haunted by danger.

Four years later, the cartel strikes again. This time, Lucki falls into a coma and is secretly relocated to Canada to recover. Jade is forced into witness protection and disappears into New York City under a completely new identity — escorted by Special Agent Melissa Greaves.

One Lucki Day is a poetic and gripping tale of fate, ambition, and resilience. It's about the legacy of love, the trauma of survival, and the fragile moments when luck runs out — and life begins anew.

The Blue And You - BITA Volume 2 - The Cop's Son Premium Edition

The Premium Edition is like the standard edition. Except the hardcover print and paper back images are in vivid color. The Paperback is also a larger size book than the 6x9 size of the other editions. These are collector editions.

Not So Lucki - Bita Volume 3

Stepping back into Luckì's world — years later, older, harder, healed and haunted by choices he thought he left behind. But love doesn't die quietly, and ghosts don't forget promises.

Not So Lucky will weave the echoes of Volume 1 and the fallout of Volume 2 into a reckoning. A man once in love, now on the hunt — circling back to what he never finished. Jade's memory lingers. New characters emerge. And the world hasn't gotten any softer.

The BITA Saga is a story of love, survival, and the systems that bend our names before they break them. From stolen kisses to gunshots in front of corner stores — these stories live where beauty meets brutality. One Luckì Day, The Blue And You, Not So Lucky

www.ingramcontent.com/pod-product-compliance
Lightning Source LLC
LaVergne TN
LVHW050922210926
848482LV00012B/500
9798349293030